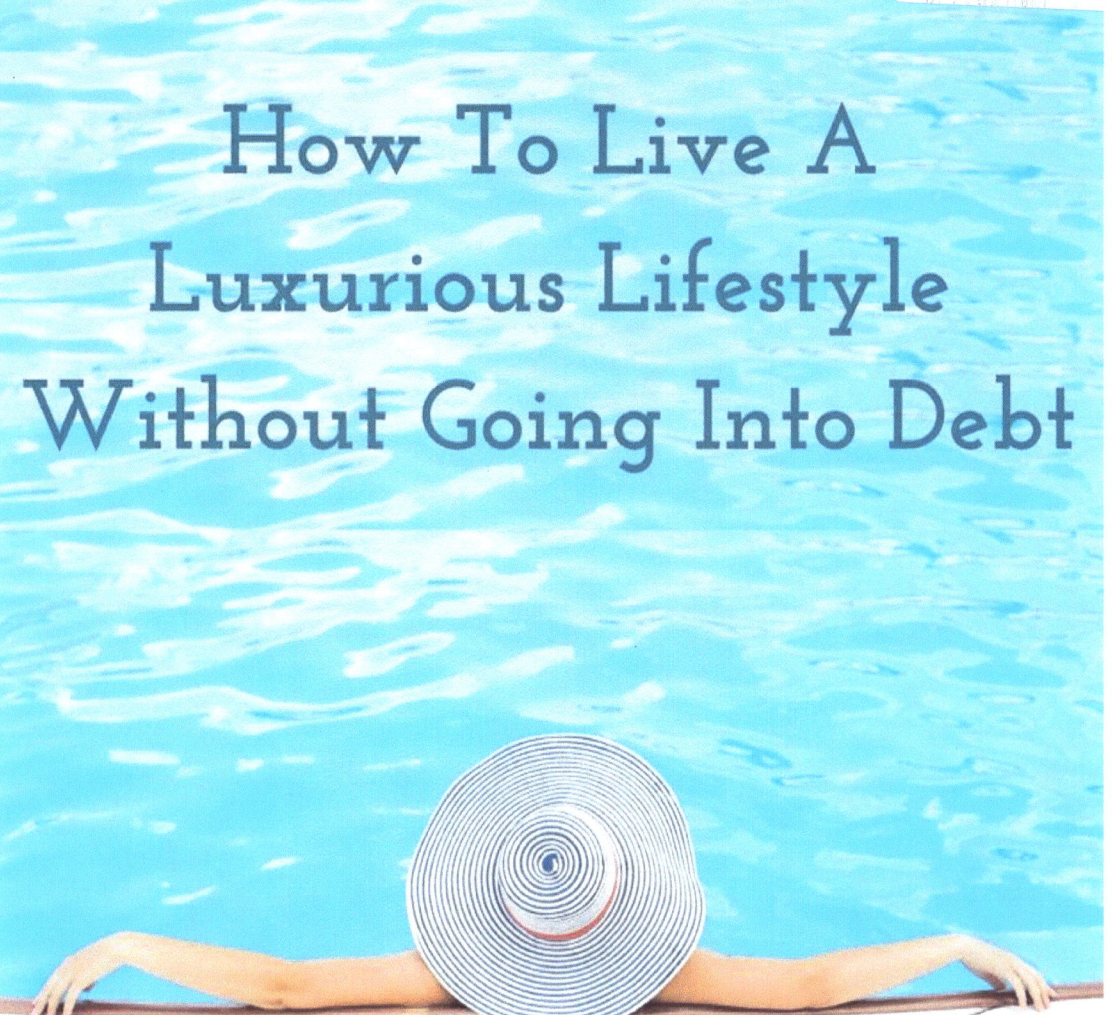

How To Live A Luxurious Lifestyle Without Going Into Debt

5 strategies you need to know in order to put more money in your pocket without over complicating it.

APRIL CALDWELL, MBA
MONEY BOSS COACH

Special Thanks to:

Kim Bynum
Toni Hernandez
Jen Devore Richter

Thank you to my Trail Blazers Tribe without you I would not know my path.

This book is dedicated to the Money Bosses I have met, not yet met or will never meet. I wrote this book to light the fire. Use that fire to start you on the path to live life on your terms and to walk fearlessly towards what you want.

I'm known as the Money Boss Coach. I am the personal CFO to executives and professionals, coaching them on maintaining a luxe lifestyle without guilt.

If you have ever thought or ever felt like:

"I can't do this alone"

"I can't change"

"This is way too complicated"

You don't have to do this alone, I'm here to help.

If you have felt any of the above, then you may understand why I am passionate about helping women. I did not wake up one day and say "when I grow up I want to be a Money Coach". Little did I know, this would become my passion in life.

I grew up in an upper-middle-class family, a nice house, a stay-at-home mom, two cars, private school and a comfortable life. When I turned 16, things changed overnight. We went to pinching pennies and eating lots of tuna fish casserole. I can remember my mom finding items in the house to return to the store and selling things to make ends meet. This continued until I moved out at 18yrs old.

This time in my life had a profound impact. It affected the way I viewed money, freedom, and survival. I knew I never wanted to be back in a position like that again.

I use my personal experience, my MBA, and over 20 years in the finance industry to help my clients work towards their goals and create a luxurious lifestyle. I am a wife and mom, an Army veteran who served during Operation Enduring Freedom, and a Jacksonville native. I currently reside in Jacksonville Beach with my husband, John and my pooch, Penelope Clementine. I call her Penny. See, even my pooch inspires me to think 'money'.

OK, enough about me. Let's talk about you.

Are you ready to have a luxurious lifestyle? ie. Brunch with your girlfriends, 5-star vacations, the dream closet.

You can have this lifestyle without feeling guilty, wondering if you can afford the things you want, if you have enough money saved, or if you can maintain this lifestyle.

I am going to teach you the T.R.A.I.L, the Trail Blazers Proven Process to A Luxe Lifestyle. These are the 5 strategies to keep more money in your pocket and live your dream life without over complicating it.

        T - Tackle Your Numbers
        R - Realize Your Lifestyle
        A- Acknowledge Your Why
        I - Implement the Plan
        L - Leverage Your Progress

I'm here to tell you that by following my 5-step strategy you will learn what you can live without, learn what is priority, and most importantly, take care of yourself and maintain the lifestyle you want.

Towards the end of the book is a page for you to take notes and jot down your thoughts.

T- Tackle Your Numbers

Let's talk about the financially sexy numbers every woman should strive for; **750-3-35-15-35.**

1. **Know your credit score and shoot for 750+**
    What's your score: _____

2. **Have an Emergency Fund**
Set aside **3**-6 months' worth of your fixed expenses. **This is your 1st financial priority.**
What is my monthly fixed expenses? _____
How many months do you have set aside: _____

3. **Keep Your Debt In Check**
Debt should be less than **35%** of your income.
My monthly net income is _____
Your debt ratio: _____

4. **Save 15-25% of Your Income**
How much depends on what style of retirement you want
My Yearly net Income is _____
Percentage you are saving: _____

5. **Your Credit Card Utilization should be 35% or lower of your total credit limits** *(add up all the balances, add all the credit limits, divide the total balance by the total credit limit then multiply by 100)*
    Total Credit Card Balance _____
    Total Credit Card Limits _____
    Your percentage: _____

How did you do? Just by taking the initiative to download this e-book and get started, you are on the right trail. Congratulations on taking the first step to tackling your numbers.

Only by knowing your numbers can you know where you currently are. Then, make small changes where you can. *Ex: if you get a raise at work, bump up your savings. Be more aware about how often you are using your credit cards and switch to cash.* It can take some work to get financially sexy but small steps will add up and take you to where you want to go!

To know where you want to go, you have to know where you are starting.

What's your total household income?
- _____

What's your monthly expenses?
- _____

Where are you spending your money?
- _____
- _____

How much are you saving each month?
- _____

What do you have left over?
- _____

Are you living your best life?
   YES   NO   ON MY WAY

Need help getting started? Download the Free Money Boss Budget Worksheet at https://www.aprilcaldwell.me/freebies

Start with a money journal.

I always start my clients with a Money Journal. Carry around a notebook and pen with you everywhere. Anytime you spend money (cash, debit or credit card), **write it down.** This will help you realize your spending vices (those things we always find a way to spend our money on) and will help you understand your spending habits.

I recently worked with a woman who was a single mom who could not figure out where her money was going. After journaling for just a few days, she discovered the culprit; her beloved pets. She was spending so much money on unplanned trips for dog food, dog toys, more dog food that it wasn't until she started doing daily tracking that she realized how much these unplanned trips were costing her. By taking control of this spending, she was able to save $200 a month.

Work on a budget. Yeah, I know. Budget is a bad word, or at least it FEELS bad. Every article you read about budgeting and saving money tells you, "Stop buying lattes! No new clothing ever!!!" but that's not the reality of your life or your new budget.

Your budget is going to help you create the life you want and spend money on what you want without guilt or remorse. It is the foundation of a strong financial plan – a plan you'll soon love because you can do it & it gets you the future you've been dreaming of.

Look at your numbers and come up with a plan. What shouldn't be an expense? Where do you need to make changes?

R - Realize Your Lifestyle

First, decide what is important to you. Do you want to take care of your family, your parents, donate to charity, have a huge savings account? Then think about all the fun stuff you want; brunches, vacations, shoes. What else do you see when you close your eyes and dream about your life?

Write down what comes to mind:

_____

_____

_____

Are you spending your money in a way that aligns with your values? Are you living the life of your dreams?

Maybe you are telling yourself that you don't have enough money, that things are too expensive for you or that now isn't the right time?

Why can't now be your time? If you haven't tackled your numbers, you won't know if you have enough money or if things *really* are too expensive. Not knowing how much debt you have, and how much you have saved for the future, just leaves you guessing about how you stack up.

Kim is a wife and mom of 2 great kids, one of which is special needs. When I met with her and her husband they had 2 priorities; make sure they could take care of their special needs son, and still have Taco Tuesday night out every week. By looking at their budget, moving some things around and switching taco night to a cheaper restaurant, we were able to make sure we achieved those goals. You can have your tacos and eat them too.

Now, assign value to what you wrote down and list them below.
My Top 3 Priorities:

- _____

- _____

- _____

My Top 3 Wants:

- _____

- _____

- _____

What you listed about is how you should be spending your money. If you are spending money on eating out when you really want to be healthy and fit, now is the time to change it. Maybe you don't realize that you are spending $400 a month on drive-thru food.

Sit down and come up with a plan to cover expenses, assess your debt and savings. Start adding in the luxury items.

Sometimes you need a reset and this is a great time for it What reset do you need? A reset from friends, from stuff or old habits, a reset on living arrangements. Or maybe you're needing a fresh start with your budget?

Realizing your lifestyle means re-accessing what it is and what you want it to be.

A - Acknowledge Your Why

You have now spent some time getting clear on what your values are and what you spend your money on.

What did you discover?

That you aren't willing to settle for a nice lifestyle by working for the rest of your life, aren't willing to greet shoppers with carts or flip burgers after you retire?

That you want freedom from financial restrictions sooner rather than later, and you're willing to do what's necessary because no other alternative is tolerable?

Once you have achieved your priorities and wants listed above, how will it impact your life? Why do you want to do this?

I believe that being a Money Boss, aka financial planning, is less about understanding hard financial concepts and more about focusing on your behavior around money. Did you discover you need to make some changes to start living authentically?

Living a Luxurious Lifestyle is not for those unwilling to make changes to their spending habits. Commitment to wealth is the realization that you'll attain financial freedom no matter what. Period.

It's not a question of "if," but rather "how" and "when".

You gain this clarity of commitment when you understand WHY you are making new choices and new changes. In the previous chapter what showed up as a priority? That is your WHY! **Write it down.**

Sally decided she wanted to take control of her money and her spending so she could focus on what was really important to her, traveling. She knew that if she wanted to take those amazing international trips that there were some things she would have to say "no" to. We created a values based budget for her that allowed her to live a luxurious lifestyle, cut out the stuff that wasn't important and say Yes to saving for those 5-star vacations. She found it so much easier to say "no" when she knew her burning "yes".

Think of your WHY as your "Hell Yes!". Then you know what your "Hell No's" are. It is so much easier to say 'no' when you know what the tradeoff is.

My Hell Yes! List:

- *Example: I want more time with my friends and Brunch 3x a month.*
- *Example: I want to create a savings account that gives me a sense of peace.*
- _____
- _____
- _____

My Hell No List:
- *Spending $250 a month on lunch I eat at my desk.*
- *Living off my credit cards waiting for it to catch up with me.*
- _____
- _____
- _____

I - Implement The Plan

Now you know your numbers: income, expenses, debt.
You know the lifestyle you want to have and WHY that is important to you.

Now, you have a really good money map, a blueprint.

Time to Implement.

Look back at the work you have done, review your responses. What are the areas you need to cut back on because they do not align with your values or priorities?

- _____
- _____
- _____

What areas do you need to give more time or money to?

- _____
- _____
- _____

Keep your answers, pull them out and review them as needed. They are what will keep you on track making the right decisions, decisions you made that will lead you to your luxurious lifestyle.

L - Leverage Your Progress

As you align your money with your values and stop spending money on the things that are not important to you, you should start to see more money in the bank.

As things start improving, now is not the time to let your Prada pump off the accelerator of your dream car.

You have to be a Money Boss and assign each of those extra dollars a job. Where do they need to go and what do they need to be doing?

Are you planning for that next vacation? Remodel? Or maybe you just want more dollars in the bank. You should be putting that money towards your priorities.

Choose one of the following and complete it within the next 48 hours. Then join our private Trail Blazers Tribe Facebook Community and let us know what step you took:

- Transfer $25 into a savings account. If you can make this a recurring transfer, BONUS POINTS FOR YOU! If you already have an automatic transfer then increase the amount by $10.
- Decide which credit card you are going to pay off and start automatic payments.
- Hire me as your money coach and start my 12 week program.

It can be scary to change the way that you have always done things, but you can do it. I believe in you!

My goal for you is that you walk away with a better understanding of your money, where you are and where you want to be.

T.R.A.I.L, The Trail Blazers Proven Process to A Luxe Lifestyle, are 5 strategies to keep more money in your pocket and live your dream life without over complicating it. Yes, a luxe lifestyle starts with a budget!

If you're one of the millions of people who struggle with putting your money to work for you, give yourself a break. If this money thing was easy, no one would have money problems. So rest easy and simply get curious about how you can approach your money and budget, differently.

You're human and you're going to get off track every once in a while. When you feel you've made a mistake with your budget, give yourself a break. Take a moment and give yourself a ton of credit! You're becoming mindful when it comes to money, and you're giving yourself the chance to succeed. That's priceless.

Working with a budget can feel uncomfortable at first, but as you move forward with it and experience little and big wins, you'll feel more motivated and empowered. You'll prove to yourself that you can manage your money well, and you'll stop spending money on things and experiences that you think will bring you happiness, but really won't.
Imagine how it will feel to have a healthy relationship with money!

Stress, Money and Health go hand in hand. Instead of letting debt rule your world, set a new standard for decreasing your debt- becoming more mindful, educated and happier along the way!

It takes most people about 3-6 months to be on a steady path of healthy financial behaviors and to be strongly planted in their Manolo Blahnik pumps, secure in their financial picture. So, if it feels like the process is slow, hang in there. It is worth it! Being a Money Boss is an inside job and can be cultivated in anyone with curiosity, determination, discipline and an open mind.

My Notes:

About the Author

I am passionate about helping people manage their money. Personally, I saw the impact money had on the women in my life. I know firsthand what it is like to have grown up affluent and then as a teenager watch my family lose everything due to poor financial planning. I rebuilt my finances through education and financial literacy which I now use to help others to reach financial freedom. I received an MBA and have 2 Bachelor Degrees: Health Management and Business Administration and have over 20 years experience in the financial industry.

Talking money can be scary. For some, it may have been a divorce, or the loss of a loved one. Sometimes it's a career change or simply a personal setback. Regardless of the issue, many are tired of feeling like a victim and want to take back control of their life.

I help people realize they need to make their financial affairs a priority in order to go from a feeling of surviving to a place of thriving. As a money coach, I like to start people off with attending an event. **The Trail Blazers Online Coaching Program**, is a 6 week live online course which gives women across the country to learn from and interact with me and other women going through the same struggles. Come meet me and a group of fabulous new friends. Together we will explore how to regain control of your finances.

Where you can find me:

Email: hello@aprilcaldwell.me

 Subscribe to my Youtube Channel: April Caldwell https://goo.gl/CvYZcn

@trailblazersrise

 @aprilcaldwell.me

Next Steps:

Visit my Website: https://www.aprilcaldwell.me
to access these Free Resources:

- Money Mindset Worksheet
- Money Boss Budget Worksheet

Join the Trail Blazers Group Coaching Program:
https://www.aprilcaldwell.me/groupcoaching/

Schedule A Money Boss Breakthrough Session Call:
https://calendly.com/april-caldwell/discovery-session

Additional Worksheets:

What's Your Money Mindset?

How would you describe your relationship with money? Include the practical stuff but also the emotions, beliefs, and more.

Did your family experience a defining moment around money?

What memories do you have of your parents discussing money?

What is your first memory about money?

Do you have any unhappy memories around money from your childhood?

What emotions did your family associate with money?

How would you define the status of your family growing up? Were they considered rich, poor or middle class?

Where are you a money boss in your relationship to money? What really works for you in this area? Where do you rock with money? What are you proud of?

What was a really tough money experience you went through? Please write the gory details. What did you do to get through this? What did you learn from it, and what are you doing differently now?

How To Make A Money Decision: B.O.S.S.Y.

Budget: Do you have enough money right now to make this purchase? If not, what do you have to sacrifice to make it happen? Is there another way to cut expenses or bring in extra cash to cover it?

Origin: Where is the want coming from? Need or Want? Have you been wanting/needing this for a long time or is it a spontaneous desire? Does this purchase line up with your values and your timing in life right now?

Significance: Is it valuable to you? Would your life be different or better with this purchase? How so?

Settling: What will happen if you don't make this purchase? Are you trading a long-term goal for this? Does this purchase align with your values?

whY: Why do you really want this? Is it an emotional or physical need? Is it a short-term fix to an emotional situation?

5 Ways to Amplify Your Financial Sexy!

Financially Sexy Numbers   750-3-35-15-35

1. Know your credit score and shoot for **750+**

2. Have an Emergency Fund
Set aside **3**-6 months worth of your fixed expenses This is 1st financial priority

3. Keep Your Debt In Check
Debt should less than **35%** of your income.

4. Save **15**-25% of Your Income
How much depends on what style of retirement you want

5. Your Credit Card Utilization should be **35%** or lower

https://www.aprilcaldwell.me

MBA, Financial Planner
CFO • FOUNDER

APRIL CALDWELL
BLAZE YOUR TRAIL

TO SCHEDULE SPEAKER, CONTACT US AT:

April Caldwell, MBA
hello@aprilcaldwell.me
904.616.0600
https://www.aprilcaldwell.me

MISSION

TO EMPOWER, EDUCATE, AND EQUIP WOMEN WITH THE KNOWLEDGE TO BLAZE THEIR TRAIL TO FINANCIAL INDEPENDENCE.

SIGNATURE PRESENTATIONS

5 Mistakes Women Make with Money

Knowing How and Why You Spend Your Money Can Improve Your Health

Budgeting - How Every Decision Can Make You Richer

Creating Your Vision on Financial Independence

Legacy: Gratitude and Impact

Core Values

KNOWLEDGE Pursue growth and learning.
FREEDOM The courage to shape a better future. A future free of fear.
FLEXIBILITY It's not one size fits all. We embrace and aggressively pursue change.
INTEGRITY Consistently candid, honest, ethical and genuine.
TRIBE Surround yourself with people who add value to your life.

Trail Blazers  April Caldwell is founder of a monthly professional women's networking group committed to celebrating trail blazers in the community. Each month, she features a leader creating impact and educates on a specific financial topic.

All rights reserved. No part of this publication may be reproduced or transmitted in any form or by any means, electronic or mechanical, including photocopying, recording, or any other information storage and retrieval system, without the written permission of the author.